SALES

GET IT RIGHT

EBEN MBHELE

RE-SKILL.CO.ZA

Copyright © 2020 EBEN MBHELE

All rights reserved

The characters and events portrayed in this book are fictitious. Any similarity to real persons, living or dead, is coincidental and not intended by the author.

No part of this book may be reproduced, or stored in a retrieval system, or transmitted in any form or by any means, electronic, mechanical, photocopying, recording, or otherwise, without express written permission of the publisher.

ISBN: 9798642064368

Cover design by: Re-Skill.co.za
Library of Congress Control Number: 2018675309
Printed in the United States of America

This book is dedicated to Siyabonga 'Bego' Sibiya. Thank you for showing me that anythiing is possible and negotiable. All we have to do is just go for it.

Thanks Mate.

CONTENTS

Title Page	1
Copyright	2
Dedication	3
WHY READ THIS BOOK	7
HOW TO USE THIS BOOK	9
WHAT IS SALES?	11
WHO ARE YOU SELLING TO?	13
WHAT DOES THE CUSTOMER WANT?	18
SHOW ME SHOW ME	23
USING THE PHONE	27
CUSTOMER COMES IN	30
KEEP IN TOUCH	33
THE DISCOUNT QUESTION	36
THE RIGHT PRODUCT	38
SWOT ANALYSIS	40
CUSTOMER FOR LIFE	42
SALES PROCESS	50
FUTURE NOW	59
FUND MY PROJECT	65
MANAGEMENT OF YOU	69

WHY READ THIS BOOK

If there is one skill that we all need to have in order to thrive in work, life and in business; that skill is sales. The lifeblood of any organization, big or small, lies in their ability to sell their products to people looking for their products or solutions. In fact, the best sale is one made to someone that does not yet realise they need your product but finds such commonsense use for it. Think here about life before Uber, Mr. Delivery, WhatsApp, Skype, Facebook, YouTube, etc.

So, let's start right at the beginning.

Who is this book for?

The best way to find yourself in this category is by defining where you are right now. Do you fall into these categories or spaces?:

- Never received sales training
- Starting a business
- Just finished school
- Stuck in a dead end job
- Never been in a sales position
- Landed in a sale position as a last resort
- Looking to change career to increase earnings
- Never sold anything
- Preparing for that job interview
- An inventor or creator

All the above and any left out, welcome. This book is for you.

So, what is my background and what qualifies me to speak about sales and selling?

I have had a very colourful adulting career spanning over 20 years. I have worked jobs ranging from waiting tables, corporate marketing, government international relations, consumer relations in alcohol and tobacco, premium car sales and portable toilet sales amongst others. I have sold most things from Range Rovers to Portable toilets. Not just sold but did it extremely well.

Along the way, I realized that there are several things that are the same regardless of the sector you are in. Certain things you do will get you the order. Some will lose you the order. Even worse, others will lose you the customer. Rather lose the order than lose the customer. The customer can always come back in future and give you another order. A lost customer is harder to gain back and often not worth the work involved. So, don't cock it up to begin with. The most common and most important thing in any sector, is to always be honest with the customer. ALWAYS. If you don't have stock, let the customer know the truth and when to expect stock. If you don't produce the item in the specification the customer wants, let them know and explain why.

Keep the customer for life, even when you change to a different sector of the market. Number 1 rule! I will get deeper into the reasons for this later in Chapter 11.

I have made most of the mistakes I urge you to avoid. Some set me back a few months in life and others set me back a few years. Some have forced me to start over in life. My main motivation in writing this book is to help you avoid the painful lessons I have learnt the hard way.

I urge you to make this book personal to you and adapt it to your personality and develop your own sales style.

Enjoy my humble offering and lessons learnt.

HOW TO USE THIS BOOK

This is not a quick read and another book read – hooray! This is a guide to keep with you and use the lessons and practice. Right from the get-go, I can say without a shadow of a doubt, anyone, absolutely anyone can learn and master *Sales* and Get It Right. All it takes is willingness/ motivation and fearless practice.

Whenever you pull this book out, grab a notebook as well. There is no rush to finish this book. Rush only to understand the basic concepts and exercises suggested. It is true that in sales, practice makes perfect. It may not seem like you are making progress at first but keep going. Even if you think you suck and do suck in the beginning; once you start, KEEP GOING!

Above all though, do the work and you will get the results. So, before you begin, set a goal for yourself. What do you want to achieve by reading this book?

- Do you want to confidently pitch an idea to investors?
- Starting a business?
- Starting your first sales job?
- Do you want to double your earnings?
- Looking for that promotion?
- Do you want to sell 1 extra car, apple, book, shoe...?

Whatever it is, you need to know where you are going. So, step 1 get that notebook and write down:

'My goal in reading this book is to _____ (fill in the blank)'

Every time you open this book, open your notebook and read this goal out loud. Sounds anal and rather irritating doesn't it? There is a psychological reason for doing this. By doing this every time, you are priming your mind to focus in on lessons that will help you achieve this goal. Reading this statement out loud also gets you focused and in work mode. Do this each time you open this book and you will see results quicker than you expect.

I recommend you buy a notebook that has a front and back hard cover. This is your companion for brainstorming and expanding ideas shared in this book and adding your own notes. Eventually, you will open and close this notebook daily, make sure it lasts and looks neat and tidy (on the outside at least).

A salesperson is every and anyone that has selling as their job. Whether it's on a daily basis or for a project, if you find yourself in a situation of having to sell an item or an idea to someone else; then you are a salesperson. Although I don't go into the details of preparing a business pitch, understanding the basics of building a customer profile and matching them to the product you are pitching are more important than the actual pitch itself. These are the building block that come way before you even think about preparing a pitch.

Let's begin.

WHAT IS SALES?

Before we get started, let's get on the same page. You have written down your goal in reading this book – check.

If you have not done this, go back to your notebook and my notes above and do this. No long drawn out goals, just one line.

Now we need to have a basic understanding of what sales is.

Let's take the most basic definition of sales. Sales is governed by the following basic principles that you need to understand:
- Demand
- Supply

What is Demand

From time to time, we all need certain things to make our lives or experiences better. Whether it's a new car, a pen, food, shoes; anything that you need or want forms the basis of what demand is. In order for you to get this thing that you want, you first need to know that you need or want this thing and are willing to take some sort of action to get it. You need to make pasta for dinner and you realise you are out of pasta. This means you need to go somewhere to buy this pasta or change your menu. If it is important enough for you to have pasta, you will demand for someone to provide this pasta to you. You and many other people who are also looking for pasta. Once there are enough people looking for the same or similar item, they have created a demand for this item.

What is Supply

Now that you have created a demand for pasta along with other people that also need or want pasta; shops realise this when more and more people come in asking for pasta. In order to fulfill this need, shops will start selling pasta to supply this demand. The shop shelves will be stocked with enough pasta to supply the demand for it. We can delve a little deeper here and start asking the following questions:

- How much pasta is stocked?
- What price is it sold at?
- What if stock runs out?

The shop will find a way to measure, over time, how many people come in looking for pasta and what price they are willing or able to pay for the pasta at this shop. Let's leave this for another book and keep things simple at this stage.

This is sales.

You need something, someone can get this to you at the right time, price and place. Sales is how well the shop can provide the correct pasta to you at the right time, price and place.

So, in order to get the basics of sales, you need to understand that your job is to get the right product, to the right person, at the right time and price.

If any of the above are not right, you have NO SALE. It is really this simple.

Sales is the art of providing the right product, to the right customer, at the right price and time.

Remember to make some notes here and ensure you understand this basic idea. You can expand the above basic idea of sales as well in your notebook – make it personal to your situation.

So how do you know who the right customer is, what the right price is and when the right time is?

Off to the next chapter to understand possibly THE most important balance to achieve in sales.

WHO ARE YOU SELLING TO?

This is the simplest yet most critical question to answer before you even start selling anything to anyone. The customer is the person that is looking for what you are selling. Really that simple. The biggest reason people fail in sales, is that they sell to the wrong person, at the wrong time, or wrong price. The art of sales is right from the start; make sure you are speaking to the right customer.

◆ ◆ ◆

<u>START HERE</u>

Ask and it is given.

It is really that simple. Spend time right in the beginning of your conversation with a potential customer asking the right questions. I cannot stress enough how important it is to ask the right questions right at the beginning. This will save you years in your career and your life.

Let's go back to the pasta example earlier:
- You wanted to make dinner and realized there is no pasta
- If you have a partner, perhaps you ask them to pop to the shops
- If your kids are old enough, you send them to the shops
- Or you go to the shops personally

In all the above instances you are still the customer. Whether you go personally to complete the sale or not, you are still the person that needs the pasta. The people you send on your behalf act as your proxy. As an example, if you want spaghetti or fettuccini, this is what they will buy or ask you for alternatives if they don't find this at the shop. They won't decide on their own what to buy if your choice is not available at the shop. You hold the key to the sale decision.

Switch yourself over now to be the salesperson. Why is it important to know who the customer is?

If I am shopping on someone else's behalf, my choices are limited, and I don't have too much room to move in terms of getting what I was sent to buy. If its spaghetti I was sent to buy, I must find spaghetti; nothing else. As the salesperson, it is important to ask this question and note the answer as it will make things easier for you down the line. As an example, if you don't have stock of spaghetti, you will know if you can offer an alternative or even a ready-made pasta dish option.

The customer is not always the person that presents themselves in front of you. Note this down in your book and just jot down various scenarios of customers. As the question directly and you will get the correct answer and start in building your customer profile.

Now, I know the pasta example is really a low involvement purchase as far as cash value and consequences of the wrong product. Replace pasta with any other item you wish. A high involvement purchase involves a lot of decision makers and a lot of money or reputation risk for the customer. If the customer buys the wrong product, it may affect their social standing or their cash flow and investment. Build trust upfront and know your product and opposition as the customer will test you on this as they get closer to deciding on handing over their money to you. The way each type is sold is different and understanding this will give you a sales advantage.

Some questions you can ask to find out who the 'real' customer is:

- Is this purchase for yourself or someone else?
  If buying for self, decisions are his/ hers alone, mostly.
  If buying on someone else's behalf, they will need more info and you may need to call the other party to run some key decisions past them.
  Beware here of delays from customer such as – I need to ask my partner; I don't know if this would look good on him/her (we will discuss simple ways to get around these objections in Chapter 12)

- Are you buying for yourself or your business?
  Personal purchases are more emotionally charged
  Business purchases are more to the specification and less about feelings

- Is this item for your home or your office?

- Do you manage this fund on behalf of other decision makers?
  If not the main decision maker, request a follow up pitch or panel. They may be sent to hear your idea as gatekeepers for the main decision maker.
  If the main decision maker, spend some time understanding and researching their other investments and things that make them tick (play golf, travel, tech investing)

- Are you responsible for making this purchase decision or will you report back to others?
  If there is a need to report back, then ensure you provide a lot of information in writing. Offer to email information to him/her and ask for emails of other decision makers so you can copy in email.
  Offer to re-present information in person to the other decision makers at a later stage. So here your primary objective is to get a yes from him/her and then meet the other people in the background as a group

- Why are you looking at product X?

Customers always do their online research before going into a shop or calling potential suppliers. Understanding their motivation will help you structure the best deal for them. Maybe the purchase is replacing an older model, so they are familiar with the brand or the old one was lost or misplaced – then you do less selling and confirm the sound decision to stick with said product or brand.

The reason could be a status decision – my boss has one or my mentor or ex-partner. Note here that a status purchase is often a 'buy at all costs' purchase. Here you are not selling the product but selling your service to make sure everyone knows this customer has made the purchase and you are their personal assistant on this product.

Make some of your own notes here on questions you have been asked in the past or that you could ask to determine who the 'real' customer is. Knowing who the customer is helps tailor your sales 'pitch' and tells you how long you will spend in getting a decision from the customer. You need to practice being bold here in asking the right questions and asking them directly. The customer is there to buy and you are there to assist them in making the correct purchase. Note the wording is not that you are there to 'sell' them the right item.

In sales your main goal is to, always, get the customer to sell the product or service to themselves. You provide information and reinforce their motivation to buy; AND make it easy for them to buy. By now I would encourage you to think about the differences between someone buying and you selling something to them. Selling implies a lot of convincing and persuading someone. Buying is the customer gathering information and making their own decision to buy. Psychologically, in the customer's mind as well, it is important that they feel like they are buying something from you and not you selling something to them. There is a certain level of accountability involved in the customer buying vs being sold something. It is always great as an ego statement for a salesperson to say they sold so many items; avoid this at all costs. Always aim to have customers that buy from you as opposed to customers you sell stuff to. You will have an abundance of repeat business from your buying customers.

WHAT DOES THE CUSTOMER WANT?

Now that we have figured out who the customer is, the next thing we need to do is figure out exactly what the customer wants. It is important to understand that the customer has done their research on your product and competitor products prior to visiting your website or store. So then 'why are they here?', you may ask. The simple answer is to look, touch and feel where possible. Research only satisfies a limited level of customer information need. The next step after research is the need to physically see and touch the desired item. Over and above this, the customer needs to validate their decision by seeking opinion and advise from an outsider.

job when presented with a customer is simple:
- Find out who the real customer is
- Find out what the customer wants
- Find out WHY the customer wants the above (what is important to the customer)
- Find out how much information the customer already knows
- Give the customer information
- Validate the information they already have
- Allow the customer to touch, see and feel the product

These are the beginnings of the customer journey. There are many other steps which I will summarise and explain in Chapter 12.

Some note taking is required here. And no, not mental notes. This is the stage where your customer realizes that you are a pro and take them seriously. Again, please use your discretion here as some items are low involvement while others are high involvement purchases. All this means is that the customer is willing to spend more time on certain items than on others. Low involvement purchases could be pasta, bread, milk, sunglasses and pens. High involvement items could be cars, furniture and home electronics. If you start taking notes for milk and pasta purchases, you will not only waste your time but will definitely waste the customer's time and lose him. The level of involvement will also be determined by who the customer is and who he/she is buying the item for.

We have discovered WHO the customer is; now to find out more about what they want and why. Use this simple format to get all the information you need to complete this step.

<u>Customer details</u>

- Who customer is
  Discussed above

- Their contact details
  To keep in touch and send any requested info
  Create a base for communication to your clients (whether they buy right now or not)

- Area they live in
  Is your product suitable for this area (maybe it's a complex or an estate)
  Proximity to your shop (servicing, repairs, measurements to fit, etc.)

<u>What customer is shopping for</u>

- State item and model
  Mental note on availability
  Mental note on flexibility for customer to change model if same features available on higher or lower option

- Colours and sizes

Why customer wants item

- Ask why they want the item
  Old model replacement
  Old car written off
  What item will be used for
  Moving to a new house so need new sofa
  Recently divorced

- Why your brand
  Repeat purchase
  Advertising campaign

Customer research

- Ask customer if they have searched for any information on your product
  Where and what did they find
  Was this enough or do they need more info
  Validate good sources for information and suggest other legitimate sources

Customer budget

- How much the customer has available to spend
  Will customer need to finance his purchase?
  Can he be upgraded
  Is he totally out of the ballpark of your product?

- What the customer will NOT spend
  This gives you a minimum and a maximum price they are willing to spend
  Opportunity to add features or subtract to meet the customer in their comfort zone

- Don't get stuck on the budget
  This area is a mental note area and not segmentation area
  Budget is a guide and not a barrier
  Personal purchases are more guided by emotions over

SALES

budget
Business purchases are more guided by budget over emotions
Link this back to who the customer is and why they are buying

Looking at the information you have now gathered above, you can start to see why it is important. You have mapped a customer motivation page telling you everything the customer already knows about your product. Now it is a simple matter of plugging the holes in the customer's information and very importantly, giving the customer an opportunity to look, feel touch your product. We will go into more information later in this book about effectively demonstrating the product to the customer.

During the process of taking the above information down, it is important to do the following:

- Ensure you are both seated
  Don't try to get this info while standing next to your product
  This is the first opportunity you get to show the customer that you are interested in them
  Make the process quick and easy

- Make sure the customer can see you asking and writing information down
  Critical as this makes the customer feel heard and appreciated
  Being seated and writing is a prelude to completing the purchase paperwork, so you are preparing the customer for the conclusion of the sale later

- Prepare a file and place these notes in that file
  You are showing the customer that you will look after their information

You are also keeping his information on file as record of your meeting

You are now closer to understanding what the customer wants. At this stage you need to read back all the information the customer has given you. This gives them a chance to change their answers and starts painting a picture for you of the product that would fit in with the customer's needs and wants.

"Mr. Smith, looking at some of the answers you have shared with me, I believe product Y may be what you are looking for. Please follow me so we can take a closer look and test out some of the ways you can enjoy product Y."

Tailor this statement to fit in with your personality and relationship with your customer. Some customers are extremely formal while others are more open to informal talk occasionally. You can still be informal and professional at the same time. Whatever the customer preference here, always remain professional.

No one buys anything so that they DON'T enjoy it. So, your statement is inviting the customer to try the product out BEFORE they buy. This is the product demonstration. We will use information you have already gathered to ensure that we tailor the demonstration of your product to what the customer has already told you they are interested in and they want to use your product for.

SHOW ME SHOW ME

The product demonstration is an opportunity for the customer to confirm that your product is the right product for them. Your role here is to use the information gathered to:

- Direct customer to the best fit product
- First show the customer how
- Then allow the customer to show you how
- Allow the customer to safely touch, measure, push and lift your product
- Allow the customer to sell your product to themselves

This part of sales takes the customer back to when they were kids. They will inevitably rush in and start pressing buttons and flipping and turning your product. Take control. Taking control started when you asked the customer to follow you. There is a way of doing this to take control – adapt it to your own style. Once you ask the customer to follow you, get up and go in the direction of your product. Don't wait. Don't keep turning to see if they are following you. If the customer feels listened to and trusts you at this stage, they will follow and will try to keep up with you by speeding up their steps. Here's what to do next:

- Slow down just before you arrive at your chosen product.

- Approach with the customer right next to you.

- Point in the direction of chosen product
  This allows customer to get a visual and hopefully your chosen display looks amazing
  Builds excitement and anticipation for the customer

- Arrive first at product and mention product by name and model

Here you are confirming the choice based on what the customer needs

Ask "how would this look in your kitchen/ garage…?"

You are getting the customer to start taking mental ownership of your product

If mental delivery does not take place, there will be no physical delivery.

- Demonstrate product

Keep it simple

Remember the customer notes on what was important to them and why they are buying. Home in on those points here.

Do not demonstrate things according to user manual. Demonstrate according to customer uses and add the basic functionality and what makes the product unique or superior.

How to turn it on

Maybe there is an auto off sleep button

Plug options

Universal plugs that other manufacturers do not have

Seat adjustments

Let customer take a seat and show them where adjustments are and let customer find their perfect seating position

Mirror adjustments

Show customer where the button for this is and let them set themselves up

Packaging

Assembly

Uses and functions

At each stage here, link back to customer use ("this is how you would adjust the mirrors and set into memory for your wife")

- Let the customer talk about how your product looks and

feels to them as they play with it

"This feels lighter than I imagined" "It's so easy to start her up" "why is there no handle on the other side?"

These are requests for extra information. It also shows a high level of interest and engagement with your product

Imagine if the customer just said nothing and nodded or just went through the motions. So, questions and customer 'thinking out loud' is a good sign.

Although the customer is talking to you and asking you these questions, what they are doing is convincing themselves that your product is perfect for them. Your job at this stage is to answer the questions and link back to what the customer stated earlier, at your desk. *"This model only comes with one handle Mr. Smith as it stays against the wall once installed. We do have a slightly bigger model which has 3 handles as well as some other features you may like. If we can revise your budget by R250, we can look at some of these options. Can I show you this model Mr. Smith?"*

This is what the customer hears – this guy/ girl listened to me about my budget. They have an option with the extra handles I want. It's only an extra R250. It won't hurt to see what else I can get on this better model. YES!

Here is what you have effectively done here:

- Shown the customer that you care about what they think
- You care about keeping their budget in line
- You care that they may get more value by paying a little bit more
- You have not pressurized them
- You made the customer a partner in this purchase
- Gained their trust by taking notes and remembering the info and allowing the customer to buy your product as opposed to selling them your product

A lot of people have the mistaken idea that salespeople just manipulate customers into buying things they don't need. It is true that there are those that do this in order to make more in commission or sales. Don't be that guy or girl that puts profit over customer. In sales, your real job is listening and pointing the customer in the direction of what they need from what you have on offer.

Remember to keep things simple. The customer does not care about all the fancy terms you use in your sales meetings and factory tours. Use simple everyday language. No fancy abbreviations and industry terminology please. It is important to note here that the customer may throw in a phrase or two of these terms. Match the customer and go along with them on these discussions and then go back to everyday talk. It is important to understand that the customer may have spent a lot of time researching your product on the internet and reading reviews. This is an expression of interest in your product and a way for them to test whether you do have some of this 'tech' knowledge and product knowledge. Match the customer at their knowledge level and then go back to normal everyday talk.

Keep reminding yourself what the objective of the product demonstration is:

- Customer needs to confirm that your product is right for them
- Your job is to provide information and guide the customer to their final purchase
- The customer buys
- You don't sell

USING THE PHONE

The phone is not a tool for you to sell your products to your client. The simple reason that you use the phone is to get the appointment and get the customer in front of you. Sales is a contact sport and as such, needs you to be in face to face contact with your customer. Nowadays, face to face includes zoom, skype or other video call type.

Here are some ways to use the phone when dealing with the customer:

WHEN YOU CALL THE CUSTOMER

Never call a customer unprepared. Never call for no reason. You must have a reason for calling the customer. Customers are people just like you and me and they too have other things to do other than think about your product or service. Action steps:

- Prepare
    Decide what your number 1 reason for calling is and write this down in your sales notebook
    'Call Rob to check if he has had discussion with his wife'
    'Let Sally know her finance has been approved'
    'Tell Sam that your new stock has arrived'
    Get information you need to share with your customer on the same page in your notebook
    Don't go into a full speech here. Short snippets will do
    Have your diary next to you with available spaces to see your customer

- Be brief
    When you call your customer, be brief and to the point
    Remember the reason for your call
    'Hi Sam. This is Harry from Shop XYZ. I am calling to update you on your finance. Are you free to talk right now or can I call you

back in 5 minutes?'
The customer will want you to give them all the information on the phone. DON'T DO IT!

- Ask for an appointment
Let the customer know which days and times you have free to meet them and discuss your news
Only give 2 or 3 options here to avoid confusion and delays
'I would love it if you can come in for 15 minutes to discuss this Tim. I have an opening today at 2pm and tomorrow at 9 am and 1 pm. Which slot will work best for you Tim?'

Don't babble. Wait for the customer to answer. The customer will choose one of the slots or suggest something else. If it suits, agree and book the appointment
'That is great Tim. I have booked this appointment with you in my diary. Please book this time in your diary as well. I look forward to chatting with you tomorrow at 9am at our shop.'

- Say goodbye and call the next customer.

You can use variations of some of the above conversation especially when starting out. It is important to see that no news was shared with the customer on the phone. We gave the customer a snippet of what we would like to meet about and then go ahead to set the appointment. The are several reasons for doing this:

- You want to increase the number of times you see the customer with great news. This moves you in the customer's mind from a stranger to someone they know and that is a bearer of good news.
- A lot of misunderstandings can happen on the phone. You want to avoid this at all costs. It can cost you margin on your deal or cost you the deal itself.
- You want to see the customer's face and body language when you deliver the news in person. You can't do this over

    the phone.
- 	You have an opportunity to conclude your sale in person

Great news! Your customer made it in. Now what? Panic and Run! Well really no need for that.

CUSTOMER COMES IN

Your job is now getting easier and easier. Follow these steps to make sure you get the business:

- You need to ensure that you meet the customer and welcome them again to your shop when they come in.
- Thank the customer for making the time to come in
- Confirm that they still have the same amount of time available. Things change and if they have, you want to ensure you do not keep the customer beyond this time frame. Respect their time.
- Get seated with the customer and make sure you have all the documents you need to discuss with the customer

You are already on the front foot by getting the customer to come in to meet and discuss what you needed to share. At this meeting, your goal is not only to share the information discussed briefly on the phone. The bigger objective is to conclude the customer sale or to gauge how ready the customer is to finalise his purchase. In a future book we will discuss sales cycles and get deeper into low and high involvement purchases. Low involvement purchases are generally concluded in the first meeting and the customer is not as invested in the outcome of the purchase.

A high involvement purchase needs a little more time either due to the amount of money being spent or the number of decision makers involved. This type of purchase has a longer sales cycle generally and may take months or sometimes years. The sales cycle is simply how long a sales transaction takes, from start to finish.

There are several tools you can use to gauge the customer readiness to buy. Here are some of them:

- During the meeting, mention that you would like to introduce them to your manager or the owner. Having spoken to the owner beforehand, you want to leave both the manager/owner and the customer by themselves while you get busy with something else. Your manager's job here is simply gauging if there is anything holding back the customer from buying. This may be price, available colours, cash not ready etc. The customer will generally share this information more at ease with your superior than with you. This could be because they like you and don't want to offend; they are not sure if your promises will be kept or embarrassed about a financial issue. Whatever the reason, your customer generally will be more honest with your superior than with you. This technique in sales is called second voicing. You are simply getting someone that is not directly involved in the sale to assess the customer readiness to buy. You can use a business partner or colleague in this role as they are strangers to the customer.

- Handle any objection that the customer may have for not buying.

'Tim, now that we have Model x available in red, can we start the paperwork so you can take her home this week?'
Customer says Yes and you have a sale and you can get the paperwork done and signed
Customer says No and you take a step back and ask more question to find out what the real delay is
'Let me make sure we are on the same page Tim. You are happy with model x in red. Is this correct?'

Ask a whole battery of these and lead back to the preparation of paperwork. If you hit all 'Yes' and are only getting a no on paperwork, then you need to ask directly why the customer is still not ready to complete the paperwork.

'Tim, we have just confirmed that you are happy with everything that you needed our product to do. Is there something that I have left out that is important to you?'

If you keep ending up at the same NO and nothing changes, then you need to back off. Let the customer know that you are available to assist further when customer is ready and are happy to do this. Thank them and say your goodbyes.

KEEP IN TOUCH

There is never a reason NOT to keep in touch with your customer, regardless of whether they buy or not. Remember that your ultimate goal in sales is to keep the customer for life; even if you lose the sale. So, sale or no sale, it is critical for you to keep in touch with the customer.

After your last meeting, it will be clear to you how ready the customer is to buy. Keeping in touch does not mean a long meeting each time.

Keeping in touch can be an email, phone call or a SMS.

The important part of the follow up is that it must be structured and be short and sweet.

"Hi Sam, this is Peter from shop PQ. Do you have 5 minutes to chat about our invisible gloves? I have some new information I would love to share with you about the new range."

Tailor this to be related to why the customer did not buy or if they made the purchase, check if your product is treating your customer well.

Under no circumstances must you call and say, 'I am just following up'. The customer knows that you are calling to follow up either by sharing more information or checking on their readiness to buy. Your customer is not stupid so don't treat them as such. If you want to know if they have decided, ask exactly this. Don't dilly dally and beat about the bush.

All your follow ups must be scheduled in your diary with a reason for the follow up. After some time, you will start to develop different segments of customers bought, not ready yet, waiting for new model, bought elsewhere, not interested. Regardless of the labels you place on your customer, you still need to keep in touch. This can be an email every 3rd month, a phone call every 2nd month, a SMS every time you have a special or even a call on their birthday.

What you are doing here is ensuring that you keep this customer for life. At any stage of their next purchase decision of similar products, you are at the top of their mind. You are opening the door for your customer to ask you for advice and send their friends to you when they are looking for your product or service. The customer starts seeing you as a subject matter expert and values your opinion and does not feel like you are just in it for the sale. You will also be able to gauge what too much keeping in touch is as your relationship with your customer develops. Trust your gut and listen to the customer feedback. Too much keeping in touch can kick you to the curb and throw you right out of favour with the customer. There is no set rule for how often you should send what type of information to keep in touch. Every person is unique, and every customer is a person; as such each customer is unique. Build your relationship with your customer and you will know when the right time to call, email and SMS is.

While technology is a great tool for keeping in touch, it will serve you well to occasionally send a handwritten note. I would recommend sending a thank you note written by hand. A 1-year product purchase anniversary should also be handwritten. Nothing expensive or fancy.

"Hi Tom. Your PT Microwave is 1-year old today. To celebrate, please pop this inside her" – Have this delivered with a pack of microwave popcorn.

I can guarantee that no other appliance salesperson is doing this. Zip. You are the only one and your customer values this more than any discount or other superpowers you may have.

All their friends will start calling you and emailing you asking for you to give them the same treatment.

How much does a pack of microwave popcorn cost?

THE DISCOUNT QUESTION

A discount is when you agree to let the customer pay a lower price than your listed price.

There is a lot of psychology linked to giving and receiving a discount.

None of these reasons are linked to the customer buying or the customer being your customer for life.

Simply put, when a customer asks for a discount, they want to check if you have given them the best possible deal. The minute you agree to give the discount, the customer knows that you did not initially give them the best deal. They may very well buy, this time, but rest assured that all future purchases will only happen based on whether you give or don't give a discount. Kiss your profit margin goodbye and say hello to having to work more for less reward.

The customer is looking for some value from you.

This is how you should interpret this request from your customer. It is simply a request for you to provide them with more value in the purchase. Value is not money. It's a question; *'what else can your product do for me?'*

The best way to deal with this is really taking a step back and re-stating all the requests that the customer has made that you have fulfilled, like the colour, delivery today, extended warranty, etc. Really go to town on how your product fits perfectly into your customer's life. This is called building value.

"Richard, I would like to make sure that I am giving you everything you have requested. We managed to secure the Red unit, are you still happy

with this?"

Customer says Yes. You need to keep going through all the customer special requests to keep getting a yes from the customer. Right at the end mention that you have given them great service and have made sure they get the perfect product to fit in with their needs. Then mention how the features of this product can add value to their life. Mention here things like auto power off as he is a busy individual, auto lights on and off so they don't have to remember to turn them on or off, standard phone navigation that alerts them to traffic on their normal travel routes and times, etc.

In short, never ever give the discount. All your future transactions will be dependent on you giving a discount. When the customer asks for a discount, they are asking you to add some value. The best way to add value is to show the customer the different ways their new product fits in to their life and makes it better. The customer needs to feel that they are receiving more value than what they are paying for.

Discount giving starts a price war and price-based value. If you sell your product and compete based on price, your sales life and your product life will be very short lived. You do not ever want to be involved in a price war, ever.

The fear in you is that you will lose the sale. It is ok to lose the sale. This loss protects you from being part of a discount price war. Soon enough your customers will know that you give great service and value and not dish out discounts.

In case it wasn't clear, NEVER EVER DISCOUNT YOUR PRODUCT.

THE RIGHT PRODUCT

I have often wondered if this exists. I am sure you have too. One customer will like their pasta al dente, another will want lots of salt, others will like it creamy whilst yet more may want it just plain. What you must understand is that the right product exists but is not a universal standard. You can't take a product, label it 'THE RIGHT PRODUCT' and frame and display it. The right product is the product that is right for a specific customer at that time. Note, it is only right in that time. Not forever.

Here is an example: recently divorced client comes in shopping for a new swimming costume. They are in great shape and are looking to get back on the market as it were. They live alone with no kids or pets. They work as a freelance blogger. You both work through all available options and finally find the perfect swimming costumer for your customer and it is a luminous green 2 piece. It is perfect. You think it is perfect. Your customer thinks it was made just for them. Congrats, you found the right product for you customer. Well, right product, right now.

A year later, your customer finds the perfect partner and settles down to start a family. A year later, they have twins and start a job as a legal assistant. A further year later, your customer then comes back to you to get another swimming costumer. Surely, since you were both able to agree on the right product back then, you can still use this same right product and just give her a newer one?

As you may have guessed, NO. big fat NO.

The right product was right all those years ago based on your customer circumstances at that time. In the present though, that product is no longer the right product for a married mother of two who is a legal assistant and starting a new life in corporate. Perhaps now something that covers a lot more and not as bright, maybe even black or dark blue in colour.

The right product is right at the moment of purchase and maybe for a while after this. Once certain critical circumstances change for the customer, your product is no longer the right product for your customer. That is the bad news.

The good news is that there is a very easy way to ensure that you get the right product for your customer each time they come in to see you. In fact, you can get the customer to be part of the selection of the right products. This golden key is something called the SWOT analysis. This simple tool is your best friend when it comes to narrowing down the options for your customer and helping them select the right product for them.

SWOT ANALYSIS

That sounds pretty fancy doesn't it?

This is the easiest and most useful sales tool out there. Have a look at the diagram below and just copy this onto a blank piece of paper when sitting down with your customer. This analysis is a simple way to match what your customer has told you about themselves to what your product can offer. A type of match making as it were. Since you cannot change the customer but can get different options for your product, this analysis is a quick view of how closely your customer needs and personality can be matched to the right product. Have a look below at the notes and what the letters mean.

SWOT ANALYSIS

S – STRENGHTS	W – WEAKNESES
- Vehicle available in automatic as per client preference - Your stove uses gas and this is the customer's preference - Our shop is near customer home or office	- Stock only arrives in a week and customer Is ready to buy right now - Product can only be assembled at the shop therefore may be a challenge to fit into client's home on delivery
O – OPPORTUNTY	**T – THREAT**
- Up sell client to model that has stop/ start technology. Can offer a higher spec to meet client needs - Customer willing to order and wait	- Opposition store launching in your area soon - Client shopping on price only so can be swayed by opposition pricing strategy - Bad media publicity

CUSTOMER FOR LIFE

I hope you have realized by now that sales is not just an easy way to make money. Sales is your gateway to an income and profession for life. If you can master the basic concepts and improve on them, soon you can be a sales master. Like any other skill and career choice, practice makes perfect. Put in the work every day in your chosen profession and the results will be phenomenal. Look at all this work as an investment in your future income and network.

The idea of keeping a customer for life is simply that; ensuring that your customer remains your customer even when you change company you work with and for, you change career paths or open a new company. Here are some reasons why you would want to keep a customer for life:

- If you open a new company, they may be interested in what your new company does
- If you change from selling lawnmowers to selling fridges, they or a family member or friend may be looking for that item now or in future
- It is easier to deal with people you know than to get new customers. Keep in touch so you can start your new path with familiar faces
- It is easier for the customer to keep dealing with the same person that they know and trust
- You have done the hard work to build a customer profile and build trust with the customer through delivering value

Put yourself in the customer's shoes for a bit and imagine buying everything from your car to your appliances and shoes from the same trusted source. Imagine knowing that you will get the same level of service when buying each of these items. There will be no awkwardness and mistrust involved in starting a new relationship.

So, what better reason could there be for keeping your customer for life?

◆ ◆ ◆

It sounds so fantastic but how can you do this. How can you keep one customer for their whole buying life? Here are some ideas that you can try and fine tune:

- Treat each sale as part of the customer buying cycle and not as an opportunity to retire rich from the transaction
 Be fair
 Don't be desperate to close the deal
 Understand that the right customer for your product will change over time. Allow for this and keep you customer file up to date

- Keep in touch
 The customer is human, and they love it when you remember information that is important to them
 Send a message or make a call for their birthday or any family member celebration and anniversary.
 Send a card on the anniversary of each of their purchases. (purchased from you and from your opposition.

 Chance are your opposition will not send this to your customer)
 This is not about spending lots of money on these reminders but simply picking up the phone and sending a handwritten note will keep your customer with you for life.
 The more occasions you create for an interaction with you customer, the stronger your relationship will get over time.

Invest in this relationship and the money will come on its own

- Lose the sale

If you have done absolutely everything possible to put together a fair, tailored deal and you still cannot get the sale; it is ok to lose the sale in order to keep the customer.

Even when your customer does not buy from you, stay interested in their purchase. Ask them where they are buying and when. Call on the day to congratulate them and express an interest in seeing their purchase and be genuinely happy for them.

It sounds counter intuitive and further bruises your ego from losing the sale but remember you are in this for the long haul and not just for the sale.

You now have a delivery date and a future celebration and reason to keep in touch with your customer. Send a message and card on the anniversary of this sale too.

The customer will be so impressed that you have a vested interest in their happiness even if you are not the source of it. So just keep building on this. The customer will start keeping your number close for advice and recommendations.

- Create a network

Regularly attend industry and various exhibitions and build relationships with the exhibitors and their salespeople. Spend some time developing these relationships with others who share the same ideas as you about how to treat and keep a customer.

Share some of this information with you customer when you keep in touch. *'I attended a gardening expo a few months back and have kept in touch with the owner of Flowers Unit, if you need really great service and a fair deal, let me know and I can personally introduce you to them.'*

You are now a source of information for your customer and a network for great service across various sectors.

Invite your customer to attend your own customer events and to bring their family and friends.

You are now extending your direct potential customers to their family and friends. They may like you even more than your customer and send you some business.

- Build a relationship with your customer's gate keeper. A gatekeeper is often the customer's personal assistant or business associate. They manage the customer's time by screening the people that get to see them.

This gives you direct contact with your customer and builds your credibility with your customer. If you can't get a hold of them for something important, you can very easily contact the gatekeeper and get the correct information across to your customer on time.

Treat the gatekeeper as if they too are your customer. Note down and remember important dates for them. Send handwritten notes invites to relevant events based on their interests.

Ensure that you are aware of the dynamics in your customer and gatekeeper relationships. As an example, your customer may not want their personal assistant attending the same events as them. You will figure these dynamics out pretty quickly and note them accordingly and keep lines clear and clean. Remember who the customer is and what the role of your relationship with the gatekeeper is.

- Be yourself

It is so tempting to make every sale to everyone. The reality though is that not everyone will like you and you will not like every customer that approaches you. So just be genuinely yourself. This does not mean being too firm and stuck in your ways but just be who genuinely are.

The energy you put out into the universe is the very same energy the universe will send back to you. Make sure it's you. Make sure it's good.

If you cannot see yourself dealing with the same customer for the next 5 years, then this is NOT your customer. Make peace with this and move on to the next customer that may be a match for you.

Treat sales like starting any new relationship. The right customer is also doing the same in their interaction with you. They are not trying to catch you out; just matching you to their personality. Sometimes it won't work out.

You are not every customer's cup of tea. Make peace with this and you will be infinitely happy and productive in your chosen career.

Be comfortable in your own skin and your customer will pick this up and this in turn helps them be more genuine and honest in their dealings with you. Energy in = energy out.

- Be honest

Honest is so rare yet so important in building a lasting relationship. Customers recognize honesty and over time have had glimpses of your true character and honesty.

If something cannot be done in the customer's expected time frame, be honest and let them know. Give them alternatives so that they can plan their lives accordingly. There can be nothing worse than expecting to take delivery of your new car on a certain special occasion only to be let done by a salesperson that has overpromised and not been honest about any hurdles along the way

- Under promise. Over deliver
  This is exactly what it is. If you expect a customer's order to take 2 weeks, promise them 4 weeks. In this way, when you deliver in 3 weeks, you are an instant super star that not only has kept their promise but has also over delivered.
  Trust

- Listen and Act right
  Each one of your interactions with your customer is an opportunity to add to your customer notes file. So, listen and take notes as soon as the customer takes leave of you.
  Not every piece of important information will be share with you in a formal manner. The customer may mention in passing that they are getting ready to move to a new house in a month's time. How amazing would it be if you called them around this time to check how their move is going? No customer expects you to remember this but the fact that you did is a huge positive in building your relationship.
  The customer will share loads of information that you can use to tailor each purchase for them and most importantly their family
  The customer mentions they are buying a new vehicle from you as they expect a new baby in a few months. How amazing would it be if you add a baby car seat as a gift when they take delivery? It may be a tiny gesture for you but a really big deal to the customer AND their family.

- Above and beyond
Your real job in sales is to be of help to your customer. Always be willing to go above and beyond what your traditional job description is. Doing the things that are classed as 'not my job' is where you will win with your customer.

Customers are human too and need assistance from time to time with things that traditionally do not form a part of the sales role. They may need to get a booking for a repair or service to their appliance. As an industry insider, you know where the best places to do this may be. Make the phone call and connect your customer to the best service providers out there.

Do the running around for your customer to make sure they enjoy the product they purchased from you to the fullest. Maybe you have information on how to help their battery last longer – share the info. It costs you nothing but means everything to the customer.

- Be the customer
When you go shopping for yourself or your family, remember to be the customer and look for rock stars out there that you can build a network with and share best practice with.

You may see things that you do in your profession that are irritating and not helpful. Adapt and fine tune your art.

You are in a unique position of being familiar with both the role of the salesperson and of the customer. This will become your real superpower over time.

The biggest realization as you grow in your chosen role as salesperson is that the bar is set pretty low. Through a repetition of poor service, the customer expects very little from the sales interaction and the interaction with your company. Just by doing the basics, you will set yourself apart from the rest in a big way.

When last did you receive a handwritten thank you note from your car salesperson? When last did your washing machine salesperson call you on your birthday? Can you remember the last time you received useful information from your laptop supplier, on how to increase your battery life?

Your answers above go to show just how low the bar in sales has been set. This will make your job easier and harder. Harder because the general customer expectation is so low, and you get frowned upon by some customers by raising the bar a little. Easier because just by doing a few little things, you become a rock star. Be very careful not to settle for the low bar. Keep raising the bar to your personal best and keep wowing the customer.

SALES PROCESS

Perhaps this should have been right at the beginning. A good thing it is right towards the end. This is a recommended process and flow of your interaction with your customer. Wrap your mind around the earlier concepts first before diving into this process.

When a customer calls in, walks in or emails your company, there is a recommended process that you should follow in interacting with them. This is also called the customer journey or steps to a sale. This is really a map of the steps that you need to walk the customer through in order to successfully conclude the sale. This sales process, once mastered through practice, will set you apart from the masses of companies and salespeople competing for the same customer.

Imagine yourself looking to make a purchase and in each step, imagine how you would like to be treated and what the next natural step feels like. A lot of what is contained in the sales process is tried and tested and proven to work. Use this as a guide to ensure that you always know what step of buying readiness the customer is at and what actions you need to take. This is important that you know exactly what you need to do at each step that you take the customer on. The ultimate goal of the sale process is the sale. And gaining a customer for life.

These steps apply to sales that occur in person and not for tele sales-based products and businesses. Although a lot of these steps are similar, the actions taken will differ due to the different sales environment.

SALES PROCESS STEPS

SALES

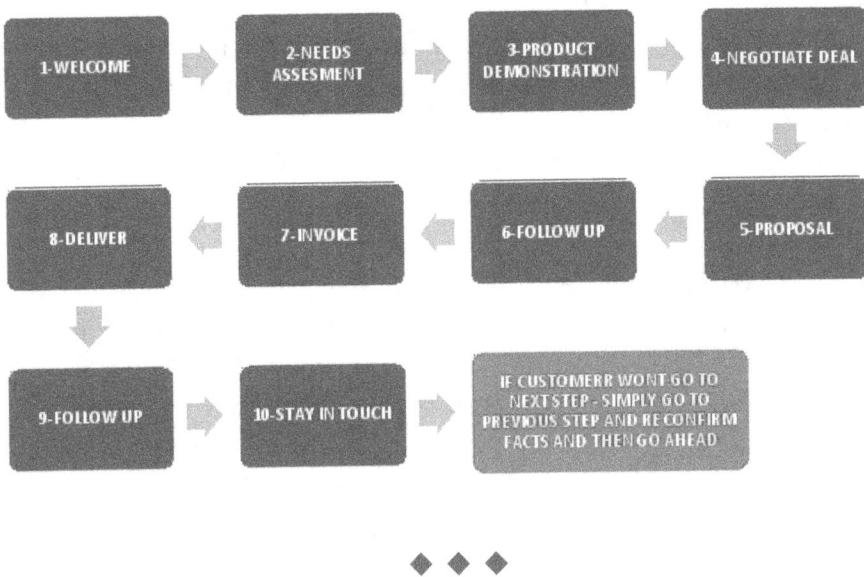

♦ ♦ ♦

STEPS EXPLAINED

THE WELCOME

You goal is securing an appointment with the customer. DO NOT SELL ANYTHING.

- This applies to a call in or walk in client
- This is the customer's first contact with you and your company so make it warm and memorable
- Before picking up the phone Smile
- Greet the customer and introduce yourself and your company by name
- Welcome the customer to your company

- Ask how you may help
- Don't ask Can I help? The answer here is either a yes or no. You want to get the client talking and need to be asking open questions
- Your main objective is to get the customer to come in to see you. Do not sell anything over the phone unless it is tele sales.
- Offer to call the client back early in the call so that you can get their contact details in case you get disconnected and for future use
- Set an appointment for the customer to come in and set a time expectation for the customer (*"Tom, for me to give you all the information you need, I will need 15 minutes of your time. Are you available to come to our shop this afternoon or tomorrow morning?"*)
- As soon as the customer confirms between the two options, let them know that you have taken your diary out and recorded this appointment and are looking forward to meeting them.
- Say goodbye and hang up

NEEDS ASSESMENT

You goal is to understand the customer motivation for wanting your product. What will it be used for and determine if the customer is the only decision maker in this purchase.

Build the skeleton of a relationship with your customer by asking the right questions.

- You have secured the customer appointment
- When the customer enters your store, repeat step 1 above, excluding parts that have to do with the phone

- When the customer confirms who they are, it is important to acknowledge that you are expecting them and are happy to finally meet them in person
- Before your customer arrives please be sure to prepare the product they are interested in – make sure it is available, visible, clean and ready to be demonstrated
- Your workspace needs to be clean and clear with just a pen and notebook on your desk. You are creating a first impression just now and a clean workspace shows the customer that you are prepared and are a professional – right or wrong, this is the impression created.
- Ensure that you get the customer to be seated at your desk so that you can gather more information to re-confirm their product choice. Never attempt to do this step while standing around the product the customer came in to see
- Follow the steps in Chapter 2

❖ ❖ ❖

PRODUCT DEMONSTRATION

You need to use the information gathered in the previous step to show the customer some options around the product you have both selected at your workstation. This may not necessarily be the same as the product they came in to see.

- Find notes in Chapter 2
- This may be the first time your customer gets to look at, touch and play with your product, so make it fun and easy for them
- Confirm that the correct product has been selected before ending this step

NEGOTIATE THE DEAL

Ensure that you both agree on timing and pricing as well as delivery.

Take control!

- You and your customer have agreed on the right product
- Now you need to put the options available and match them to price the customer is prepared to pay
- Will the product be standard, or will the customer add options?
- When is the customer expecting to take delivery?
- Ensure that you agree with the customer on the above and diarize and set appointments
- Be firm and honest especially on price and available time to finalize the delivery to your customer
- Make best practice recommendations to the customer
- Ask the customer to wait for a few minutes while you compile a proposal for

COMPILE PROPOSAL

This is a written proposal that summarises your discussion and items and price points agreed on in previous step.

- If the customer was able to wait, first thank them for waiting before you start discussing the proposal
- If the customer could not wait, give them a call and ask them to come in to discuss proposal. Never discuss over the phone. It is easier for the customer to say NO over the phone than it is in person.
- Ensure all the relevant points discussed above have been covered in your proposal

FOLLOW UP

Objection handling is critical as you either close or lose this deal at this stage. Re-state the whole deal and prepare the paperwork for customer signature.

- The norm to follow up is within 24 hours of finalizing the proposal with the customer. However, it is more important to agree a follow up when you complete the above stage – *'If I give you a call tomorrow at 2pm, will you have made a decision either way Tom?'*
- Expect some delay tactics from your customer; ranging from needs to discuss with the wife, to waiting for annual increase letters.
- Valid as they may be, every objection means there is still some level of indecision or resistance from the customer.
- Gauge how genuine the delaying excuse is and offer to assist. Maybe arrange a meeting with the partner and re demonstrate the product to both. This is the preferred route from the beginning but often not possible.
- At this stage if there is still resistance, go back to the qualification stage and confirm the customer buying motivations and re-confirm specification. What often happens when you do this, the customer will either change something you are repeating to them or they will say yes to everything.
- Right at the end then is where you confirm that you have met all their requirements. Ask is there a reason I have missed that is holding you back? The answer is yes or no. If they say yes, then get the reason and address it if possible. If a no then ask *'I am so relieved I have addressed all your needs from my product. Can I go ahead and prepare the paperwork so you can take your baby home as soon as possible?'*
- This often seals the deal. If the customer is still resisting,

give them some time and do another follow up.

❖ ❖ ❖

INVOICE

You are now at the business end of your relationship. Be firm and friendly

- Prepare the paperwork
- Ask the customer for any required documentation to complete the paperwork (finance docs, proof of address and such)
- Get the customer to sign your quote and present them with their invoice for payment or to submit to finance
- There should be no further hurdles here, barring rates and finance issues.
- You have done all you can and it is now a waiting game
- Decide on a fair time and date to prepare to deliver your product to the customer, finance

❖ ❖ ❖

DELIVER

A new baby is joining your customer's family – make this a special day for the whole family

Remember to ask if the family will be coming in to take delivery of the new car, fridge or whatever your product is. In this way, you can ensure there is enough seating for everyone and you can make this a family delivery by having a little something special for each member – sweets or snacks for kids, fancy bag holder for the wife, travel bag for the partner, etc – nothing expensive. It is about the experience.

- Always confirm a day before that things are still on track for delivery or collection

- Prepare your product and ensure this is a special day for your customer
- Pull out all the stops to make this a memorable day for your customer and their family
- You may have delivered thousands of your product, but this is the customer first or second time. Make it special
- Take lots of fun snaps for the customer – not necessarily for social media. Send these to the customer the following day with a fun caption
- Everyone values memories and this has just gone into great memories file in the customer's mind

FOLLOW UP

The customer feels valued when you still contact them after you have made the sale

- You are not done yet
- Call the customer a day later to check how their first day with your product has been so far. Have they tried that special spin feature or the handsfree phone kit....
- Thank your customer and invite them to contact you if there is something they may have forgotten or are struggling with
- Be available when the customer does contact you

STAY IN TOUCH

Keep your customer for life.

Ask for referrals.

- You have done all this hard work, don't cock it up by putting the customer file in file 13
- Schedule to keep in touch on a regular basis. You will know by this stage whether this is monthly or quarterly or biannually. Whatever it is, KEEP IN TOUCH
- A month after delivery is a safe time to ask the customer if any of their friends are looking to enjoy the same service that they received from you. Ask for referrals looking for your product
- If you don't ask, you won't get

FUTURE NOW

As I write this book, we are almost a month into lock down due to Covid19. A natural thought is pondering how sales life will change post Covid19. It is difficult to predict this but life post Covid19 will certainly be very different to how we have known it to be in the past. Sales is a contact sport and avoidance of Covid19 dictates that we practice social distancing and limit close contact. So how do you play a contact sport without contact? I have put together some ideas of how you can adapt your sales approach in your business to not only survive, but to thrive post Covdi19. All the pipe dreams of what we will do in the future have had to be actions we need to take immediately in order to stay afloat and to thrive. The future is now.

Let's first understand some of the reasons why we need social contact in sales:

- A handshake is an energy transfer and a way to establish trust and integrity

- Handshaking, fist bumping, and high fives also set the tone of your interaction with your customer. The customer normally takes the lead here

- Hugging is a transfer of energy and show of gratitude beyond words

- Face to face meetings allow us to read the customer body language and use as a confirmation of buying signal. Allows customer to also get information at the same time as having a look and feel of your product.

Visual product inspection and taking delivery.
Talk through quotes and information without the worry of spending too long on the phone.

- Eye contact is part of a social power game of and shows level of interest and respect to some extent

- We use someone else's physical presence to block off that time as a meeting and ask not to be disturbed

These are just some of the basic instances of social face to face contact and need for interaction in person.

How many of these are actually necessary? Here are some ideas of how you can adapt your business to thrive post Covid19:

- Technology bridges the gap.
Get back to basics of phone, email and SMS etiquette.
What to say when speaking to someone on the phone. How to be professional on the phone. Cut the slang out of your emails and keep your emails short, professional and to the point.

Invest in video chat apps.
Video chat is the next step after phone and SMS chats.
You would still need to block off some time to have this video meeting.
Still face to face but not in person. So here you can still see the customer's body language and facial expression.
Do your own research on the best apps for this, ranging from WhatsApp to Skype to Zoom.

Use your website as a platform to have human interaction with the customer by using website chat applications and WhatsApp contact. This can be a simple application to integrate to your existing business. Most companies currently use chat bots to interact with the customer on their website.

Load product demonstration videos on your website and social profiles. Do simple videos walking the customer through your basic products with info on their unique selling points. This can and should be personalized and sent to each customer based on how you have assessed their needs. *'Tom, I will send you a personalized video today talking you through how our product addresses your needs.'*

- Commute no more.

Do you still need to work from an office? If so, why? Maybe your office can be converted into a storage warehouse for your inventory. You may still get a few customers walking into your shop, but can you justify the rental you pay just to have one or two customers coming in every week? Re-negotiable your lease and your space. Scale down on the fancy and scale up on the practical.

Your productivity will skyrocket. You no longer need to travel to your customer's office or even your own office. The average salesperson spends more than 40%-60% of their day travelling to meetings. Now you just sit down and start dialing. You immediately have 40%-60% more time available to spend on your customers.

Re-negotiate your salary and work environment. Do you need to be in an office, or can you work from home? Bear in mind that it takes a huge amount of motivation and discipline to work remotely and in isolation. Think about re-negotiating your salary down and reduce your total days worked to at least 3 per week. You can use the extra 2 days as a freelance online consultant or sell other products online.

◆ ◆ ◆

Become a freelance online sales consultant. So, you can partner with a web developer and approach a hand full of clients that you want to work for. Get them to install online chat on their websites. You get product knowledge and have your pulse on the available stock daily. As customers look for info on a website, you are available to answer any immediate questions and send quotes on the spot. Log your leeds and put them through the sales process explained in Chapter 12.

◆ ◆ ◆

- Task Based vs time based.

The goal is for you to complete a set number of tasks per day. The goal is not to complete a set number of hours per day. So, start becoming task based. Set a goal each day of which tasks you need to complete for that day. Give them 100% and once you are done, the rest of the day is yours to do as you please. Deliverables are the new currency.

Team and project management software such as Monday.com and Asana.com are good to familiarize yourself with. Armed with your knowledge of how these can best fit your work environment will make the difference between you gaining the remote working freedom and having to continue to be office or road based. These systems simply help teams collaborate across different locations and team deliverables. You have your tasks to do and so too do others in your team. Some tasks are interdependent while other are standalone tasks. Find tutorials on these and find ways to customize these to your situation.

◆ ◆ ◆

- Adapt and Diversify
  Certain sectors will be depressed for a very long time such as restaurants, events, face to face training, and any industry that needs group or individual face to face interaction. If you are in these sectors, adapt and diversify.
  Think of ways to offer the same services in an online or distance-based manner. Virtual events, online training and seminars. Add delivery to your restaurant business. Re-negotiate your space and offer distance dining innovations with seat spacers and tabletop ordering systems.
  Add de-fogging and sanitizing stations for your patrons. This will make the customers that do come to your establishment, feel safe and cared for.
  Research sectors that are in high demand are sustainable at the moment. Find products and services that can add or diversify your business. Do your homework and research into compliance issues and legal requirements. There is an opportunity to keep your doors open by adding a new source of income to your stable.

There are many ways to skin a cat. Tons of new ways to do the same things more effectively. Apply your mind and dream. Write down all the possible barriers to the sale and think of ideas that could cut right through this. Companies have taken a huge financial hit during the global lock down therefore the opportunity is there for those that will take the bull by the horns. If you are looking to get into sales right now, you have the great fortune of having a fresh pair of eyes and fresh thinking. You have what is often referred to as beginner's mind. This is the mind that does not know the right or wrong thing and just goes more on instinct than instruction. This will be the ace up your sleeve.

❖ ❖ ❖

Familiarize yourself with some technology that provides solutions to the above challenges. Use these daily where possible. Soon you will be the expert and can use this as a new age sales skill. Keep an eye on media and recruitment ads – work remotely – familiar with skype or zoom – does not require supervision – task based – problem solver - great phone etiquette are all skills that will become necessities.

FUND MY PROJECT

It is important to bear in mind that when starting a business, you become the number one salesperson for your business. No one else understands your product better than you do. Pay attention to some of these points and think carefully about getting your business or project funded. When you come up with that brilliant product or idea and want to take it to market, very often, the first thought is that you need funding to make this happen. You need money for the website, the app, the new logo, money to pay developer and so forth. Maybe you do need an investor. Maybe you really don't.

Some things to consider before going down this route of inviting a stranger to be a part of your company:

- Do you need funding?
    After running all your numbers of doing a launch, getting that developer, office space and the lot; you must really feel overwhelmed. Here's how to work this out. What is it that will bring money into your business? Are you selling subscriptions? Is it a physical or digital product you are selling? Is it a solution to a problem?
    Whatever your business, start with the customer first. Work this part out before looking for or thinking of funding. Who is my customer and what am I selling to them?

    Can you pre-sell your offering to a set number of people that would bring in enough money for you to be profitable? Then do it. Draft what is called an off-take letter. You can take this to most corporates that will find your product attractive. The letter says, if I can successfully do ABC, will you, company A sign up? Get the letter signed and get as many of these signed. These letters will have a retail offer price and each client signs that if your product is as you have promised, they are on board.

Put all the letters together and start adding the numbers. Take this to the bank along with your proposed costs to deliver this. Most banks will advance you this start up cash as a loan. Scary right. Just think though what you have done. You have presold your idea and cashed the money upfront to realise the end product, without giving away even a percent of your business.

Another way to use if you have a direct customer business is to spend a little money to set up a website landing page with basic info on what your offer is. You then have a sign-up form on this basic landing page to encourage potential customers to pre-register for your launch. Buy some Facebook ads targeted directly at your potential clients. This whole part can cost under R2000. What this does is gives you an idea of the type of traction you may get when you launch. Additionally, you get to grow a base of people interested in what you have to offer. You can then communicate and keep these people up to date with progress.

A reason most banks and most corporates will go for this approach is that you have done the hard yards in recruiting your desired clients upfront. All you need is the minimum viable product. This is key. Don't go fancy and start with a bells and whistles model of your business. Promise to deliver and onboard clients in stages so that they too can pay you in stages. Even if they don't pay you in stages, go back to your initial clients as soon as you have a minimum viable product and give feedback and keep them excited. Get them to recommit to your project by re-signing your off-take agreements and signing off that stage 1 is completed according to their satisfaction. More than anything, this tells you and the bank that you are moving in the right direction.

Stay away for as long as possible from taking on a funding partner in your business, especially if all they bring is money. With money they will want controlling interest in your business, which is only fair. You have an idea, but they have the money to bring your idea to life.
Do you see yourself getting along with this partner in five years' time?
If No, then this is not the right partner

- Research crowdfunding platforms.
  Depending on your idea or project, these may be a fit for you as there is a level of control and creative freedom. So crowdfunding is similar to you getting the off-take letters upfront excepts here you find all the people that may be interested in one place.
  Crowdfunding gives away a percentage of your business in return for funding and giving the investor either perks or certain returns at a certain stage. Most projects a very future forward and are attractive investment opportunities for those looking to support and invest in startups.
  Do your research on the right platform for you

- How long will it take to get my idea off the ground with this funding?
  Whatever number you come up with, double it. There are often tons of things you don't see nor think about when you are in the excitement of the idea coming to life. If you think

it will take 6 months, it will likely take 12 months.

If you think you will turnover R100 000 in 6 months, half the amount and double the period. Yes, your idea may be amazing, but the world isn't just twiddling its thumbs waiting for your idea, in most cases. You will need to put in tons of work to get your business on the go and turning some sort of a profit

In many cases you will find that you don't need any funding at all. All you need to do is get started. Go and meet your target clients and get those off take letters signed. You end up owning 100% of your business and have done a lot of the future work in recruiting customers upfront. Try it. Thank me later. Even if you do this and then decide to look for funding, don't you think your business is more investable as one that already has signed clients just waiting for you to launch really.

Do the hard work of finding your customers at the start and the rest of your business journey will be amazing. You have already shown that you know your customer and have got them signed up already. No one can question your commitment to your project. You have proven the concept to yourself as well.

MANAGEMENT OF YOU

Whether you are the salesperson in your own business or employed as a salesperson at another company, you need to treat your sales job like a business. Never treat sales like just another job. Your company and your employer depend on your sales to keep their doors open for business. If you get the basics of sales right and excel at sales, you will make money hand over fist, so managing yourself is extremely important and a good starting point.

How do you treat your job like a business?
- Be professional, always
- Understand the numbers around your product (cost of product, sales margin, sales profit)
- Don't discount your product just to win the customer. Understand your numbers
- Spend money to develop yourself, like buying books to improve your skills and self-development
- Invest in advertising your services to get business. Don't rely on your employer or someone else in your own company to generate sales leeds.
- No leeds, no sales, no money, no company
- Build simple systems to follow up on leeds and assign and rank accordingly
- Record all costs you incur on each client and reflect this in your cost sheet per sale. Don't leave money on the table

All the above is good and well but pretty meaningless if you cannot manage yourself to start with.

Managing yourself means running your personal life like a business:

- Do you know your numbers?
- Manage your debt
- What is your monthly break even?
- What is your 5-year plan?
- Simple budgeting
- Time management

If you can master these elements in your personal life, managing these in a business become second nature.

If you are thinking of starting a business and you are deep in debt, rather get a job and learn to manage your income and expenses first. Your business is an extension of yourself and whatever happens in your personal life, will always affect your business.

If you are constantly getting yourself into financial problems, this will distract you from being the best at your sales job. Start by doing an honest audit of your personal affairs and set limits and budgets for yourself. Once you can successfully manage this in your personal life, you will be able to do this in your sales business.

KILL DEBT

There are many theories out there about how to go about killing debt. Having done this several times, let me share what worked for me. Being in debt simply means that you are spending more than you are earning. This debt could be in the form of loans, overdrafts, credit card etc. Most of these may be at legal stage with the company or handed over to attorneys for collection from you.

Get a notebook out and draft a plan covering the following:
- Make a list of all the companies you owe money. List name and amount. Don't worry about interest rates at this stage.
- Compile a simple budget explained in the next section. The only expenses you must reflect are your necessary ones like rent, food, school fees. All loans and credit especially ones that are now at legal or attorneys should be left off this budget.
- Choose the lowest debt amount and mark this as first one to go. Follow this by the next lowest and so on until you are done.
- Draft a general letter and send via email to all the companies that want their money from you. In this letter be transparent and specific. Let each company know how much money you are bringing in and how much you will pay them each month. Don't send as a bulk email – one by one but keep the letter the same.
- In this letter list all the companies and amounts owed and state which one you will start with and for how long.
- Being in debt means that you have either been ignoring the companies you owe or have not had the income to pay them. State that you do not have enough income right now to pay all of them at once.
- You will need to 'find' this money somewhere. Eliminate eating out, anything not in your budget and impulse buys. You will be surprised how much extra money you find doing this. It is going to be tough but have the goal of killing your debt in mind and remember to write it down.
- Most will come back to you and demand a higher repayment. Simply restate what you said in your letter and do not budge. Let them know your proposal is the maximum you can afford.
- Whether the companies you owe reply or not, start making payments on the dates you promised. This is your plan to kill debt and should not depend on the companies. Remem-

- ber to put this amount in your budget every month.
- DO NOT TAKE ON ANY MORE DEBT.
- This may take a year or two or more depending on how deep you are in debt. Hang in there. This is a tough lesson on living below your means and sticking to your plan. Eventually you will be done and debt free.
- The reason this works is that the companies you owe would rather get something than nothing from you. It is also a big motivator to you as it represents a plan of action and in time you will start seeing the results. Having a plan is hard to argue with and shows that you have given this some thought and are committing yourself to honoring your commitment to your debt.

◆ ◆ ◆

- Sample Letter

To Whom it May Concern

I have found myself over indebted to several companies including yours. The amount of money I earn can no longer cover my monthly minimum commitments to you. My current total income after living expenses is R1000. I currently owe the following companies: (list all companies here)

I am committed to settling the amount I owe to your company in full as per the below plan.

I can pay an amount of R800 per month until fully settled in the order listed below:

(list in order from smallest balance.)

While I understand this is not in line with our original agreement, I plead for your understanding as some of my circumstances have changed since taking on debt from you.

I am fully committed to repaying all my debt with you.

Thanks.

Regards,

You get the general idea. Adapt this to be in your own language and make it sincere. Don't get yourself into debt again. Live below your means. Spend less than you earn.

SIMPLE BUDGET

Here is a simple budget. The basics are listing all your income streams, all your expenses. Your expenses need to be less than your income, otherwise you will start incurring debt to feed your expenses. You never want to be in this position of working to pay your debt. That is no life at all.

Monthly Budget

Income – R10 000

Less: Expenses: R9000

Rent – R3000

Car – R1500

Cellphone – R1000

Groceries – R2000

Savings – R500

Education - R1000

Expendable Income – R1000

Self-management is the backbone of your success as a salesperson. It will help you keep the money you earn, instead of wasting it all.

I hope you have enjoyed this my reference guide as much as I have enjoyed putting it together.

Probably one of the most important things in sales and business is learning to manage yourself. Everything else just flows from that.

Be kind, first to yourself and then to others.

You are destined for sales success. Put in the work and keep going!

If you practice the above on each customer you interact with, over time you will start seeing more and more customers wanting to work with you. Over time you will see more and more money in the bank. You will find that with perfect practice, you become a master of your destiny and a champion salesperson.

Good luck and thank you for taking the time to invest in your career and business.

www.ingramcontent.com/pod-product-compliance
Lightning Source LLC
Chambersburg PA
CBHW070309220526
45465CB00004B/1816